MW01118382

How to Celebrate a
MESSIANIC
PASSOVER SEDER
A Haggadah הַגָּדָה
שֶׁל פֶּסַח

Rabbi Jacob Rosenberg PhD

Updated Spring 2022

Adat Hatikvah Messianic Synagogue
200 Lake Cook Rd
Deerfield, IL 60030
www.adathatikvah.org

Scripture quotations marked CJB Complete Jewish Bible: an English version of the Tanakh (Old Testament) and B'rit Hadashah (New Testament) (1st ed., Jn 6:53). Clarksville, MD: Jewish New Testament Publications. Stern, D. H. (1998).

Scripture quotations, marked ESV, are taken from The Holy Bible, The Holy Bible: English Standard Version. (2016). (Ex 31:12–17). Wheaton, IL: Crossway Bibles. Used by permission. All rights reserved.

Scripture quotations, marked NASB, are taken from the New American Standard Bible ®, Copyright © 1960, 1962, 1963, 1968, 1971, 1972, 1973, 1975, 1977, 1995 by The Lockman Foundation. Used by permission.

Scripture quotations, marked NIV, are taken from The Holy Bible, New International Version ®, NIV ®, Copyright 1973, 1978, 1984, 2001 by Biblica, Inc.™ Used by permission. All rights reserved.

Scripture quotations marked TLV are taken from The Holy Bible, New Living Translation, Copyright© 1996. Used by permission of Tyndale House Publishers, Inc., Wheaton, Illinois 60189. All rights reserved.

ISBN: 9798435428971

# CONTENTS

Understanding the Passover Seder
  Introduction   iv
    Key Word Glossary   vi
    Themes of Passover   vii
      The 4 Cups   vii
      Focus on Children   viii
      Slavery & Freedom   ix
      Salvation and The Messiah   x
  What You Will Need   xi
  Cleaning out the Leaven, Crafts & Special Effects   xii

Celebrating The Passover Seder   13
    Cleaning out the Leaven   14
    Painting the Doorposts   14
    Questions   15
    Lighting Candles   16
  1st Cup: The Cup of Sanctification   **17**
    Blessing the Season Shecheyanu שהחיינו   17
    Washing Hands Urchatz ורחץ   18
    Dipping Parsley in Salt Water Karpas כרפס   19
    Bitter Herbs Maror מרור   20
    Charoset חרוסת   22
    Plagues of Eygpt   24
    The Passover Lamb Qorban Pesaḥ קרבן פסח   25
    The Matzah Yachatz יחץ   28
  2nd Cup: Cup of Deliverance   **28**
    It would Have Been Enough Dayenu דינו   29
    Eating the Meal Shulchan oreich שלחן עורך   30
    After the Meal: Afikomen אפיקומן   31
  3rd Cup: The Cup of Redemption   **32**
    Yeshua's and the New Covenant   33
  4th Cup: The Cup of Praise   **34**
    Hallel Psalms הלל   34
    Next Year in Jerusalem!   35

Feast of Unleavened Bread and Counting the Omer   36

UNDERSTANDING THE
PASSOVER SEDER

INTRODUCTION

This Haggadah (or telling) is a practical guide for anyone who wants to celebrate Passover. While the design is primarily for non-Hebrew speakers, it will also introduce you to key Hebrew terms and ideas that can become important concepts in your relationship with God. All the Hebrew words are transliterated and translated so anyone can pronounce the blessings and enjoy the liturgy.

There are many Haggadahs, some longer and others shorter, but this one focuses on telling the story of the original Passover and how it is fulfilled in the Messiah Jesus (Yeshua). While it uses some modern Jewish traditions to tell the story, we believe they will only serve to understand the deeper roots of your faith and relationship with Yeshua. Some of these traditions can be confusing, so we have changed the order to help tell the story for modern people.

Why is this Seder different than other Seders?

The order of a Passover Seder is very traditional; however, it assumes that you follow Jewish practices every other night. So some of the traditions are designed to make people ask the question, "why is this night different from every other night?". However, this might be lost on modern readers. So we have changed the traditional order slightly to make the story the primary focus while still maintaining the "out of order" feeling of this very different meal. Each part of the story has a symbolic element that corresponds and creates a taste and smell to enhance the storytelling. In addition, if you have celebrated Passover before, you may find certain things missing. You can take away and ad what you want, but our purpose is fulfilling the commandment to tell the story.

Who can celebrate Passover?

We believe celebrating a Passover meal is found in both the Old and New Testaments and is vital for everyone. Passover is the context for Yeshua's famous words, "Do this in remembrance of me." (Luke 22:19 NIV) Later, Rabbi Paul encouraged the congregation in Corinth to "keep the Festival, not with the old bread leavened with malice and wickedness, but with the unleavened bread of sincerity and truth." (1 Cor 5:8 NIV) Therefore, this guide was written to be used by both Jewish and Gentile believers in Yeshua. Celebrating Passover gives essential context to the larger story of salvation through the Messiah. It helps us understand the extent of His sacrifice as our Passover Lamb and the power of His resurrection.

We hope that you will use this guide as a way to develop your unique Seder meals each year as a part of the lifecycle of your family, churches, or congregations.

KEYWORDS GLOSSARY

Yeshua HaMashiach: Jesus The Messiah

Afikoman: A Greek word meaning "that which comes after" or "dessert" some say it means "he came"

B'rakhah: The formula at the beginning of most Hebrew Blessings that means blessing.

Chametz: Process of leavening or food mixed with leaven that is prohibited on Passover and Feast of Unleavened Bread

Charoset: A sweet, dark-colored mixture of fruit, nuts, wine, and spices.

Haggadah: "telling" or the book used to lead the Passover

Karpas: Vegetable on Passover, usually parsley or celery

Maror: Bitter herbs, often horseradish

Matzah: Bread made without leavening an agent

Pesach: Passover

Ruach HaKodesh: The Holy Spirit

Seder: Ritual order of service

Talmidim: The Hebrew word for disciples

Tanakh: This is an acronym often used to mean Torah, Prophets, Writings

Torah: Five books of Moses or the Hebrew word for "law/ instruction."

Pronouncing Hebrew

'ch' and 'kh' have a throaty sound like German 'ach.'

'g' is always hard like a "game."

'h' is silent when at the end of a word like 'Sarah.'

'a' sounds like 'ah.'

'ai' sounds like 'eye.'

'e' sounds like 'e' like in 'bet.'

'ey' sounds like 'ay.'

'i' sounds like 'ee.'

'o' sounds like 'o' in 'so.'

'u' sounds like 'oo' as in 'moon.'

' is a stop in a word

THEMES OF PASSOVER

Passover has some important themes that you should keep in mind as you lead your Seder. Each one can affect the participants in different ways. Please pay attention to these various themes: they may affect you differently each year.

THE FOUR CUPS

The cups of wine are the overall outline for telling the story: They represent the keywords God promises in Exodus.

> "Say, therefore, to the sons of Israel, 'I am the Lord, and **I will bring you** out from under the burdens of the Egyptians, and **I will deliver you** from their bondage. **I will also redeem you** with an outstretched arm and with great judgments. 'Then **I will take you for My people**, and I will be your God; and you shall know that I am the Lord your God, who brought you out from under the burdens of the Egyptians. 'I will bring you to the land which I swore to give to Abraham, Isaac, and Jacob, and I will give it to you for a possession; I am the Lord.' " (Ex 6:6–8 NASB)

We call these cups:

1. The Cup of **Sanctification**
2. The Cup of **Deliverance**
3. The Cup of **Redemption**
4. The Cup of **Praise**

The New Testament also uses these cups as context for Yeshua's Passover Meal; Matthew 22:26:29, Mark 14:23-25, Luke 22:17-20. Yeah uses the Cup of Salvation when he declared, "This is the new covenant My blood…" (Luke 22:20)

FOCUS ON CHILDREN

The Bible always has in mind our children. God tells us to teach all His commands "…carefully to your children, talking about them when you sit at home, when you are traveling on the road, when you lie down and when you get up…" (Dt 11:19 CJB). Yeshua told us, "Let the little children come to me, and do not hinder them, for the kingdom of heaven belongs to such as these." (Mt 19:14 NIV)

Passover is a unique event in the past that is also happening as we celebrate, and the future as we pass it on as a living memorial. The Torah is clear; God commands that we "tell" this story to our children. (Ex 13:8). All of God's appointed times are supposed to teach us that God is, "…The LORD [our] God." (Lev 23:43)

However, Seder meals are considered boring, long, outdated. It is up to us to make sure our children understand the story as their own, which they will pass down to their children when we are gone. Proverbs tells us, "Train up a child in the way he should go, Even when he is old, he will not depart from it. (Pr 22:6 NASB)

We include children in the traditional meal by cleaning out the leaven before Passover, asking the four questions, finding and redeeming the Afikomen. There are so many more ways we can connect to our children through the sight, smell, and tastes of Passover.

In this Haggadah, we will use this symbol to suggest creative ways to enhance the Seder for children in the margins. These are only suggestions; above all, be creative and make this night different from all other nights!

SLAVERY AND FREEDOM

A critical theme in Passover and the Torah is remembering that we were slaves, but now we are free. Freedom is a reality we need to learn to live in; it is our identity and defines how we treat others. "But you shall remember that you were a slave in Egypt..."(Dt 5:15; 15:15; 16:12; 24:18, 22)

So during the Seder we say "Avadim hayinu hayinu. Ata b'nei chorin. Once, we were slaves in Egypt. Now, we are free."

SALVATION AND THE MESSIAH

As you celebrate a Seder, you will find many allusions to freedom from Egypt and through a future Messianic redemption. For example, even though Elijah is not a part of the Exodus story, he is an important tradition in the Passover Seder. Maybe Elijah is in the story because Malachi said, "Behold, I am going to send you Elijah the prophet before the coming of the great and terrible day of the Lord." (Mal 4:5 NASB).
In addition, the prophet Isaiah prophesied that one day the Messiah would "proclaim liberty to captives And freedom to prisoners..." (Is 61:1), but this time He would set us free from our sin. Later Yeshua said, "If you continue in My word, then you are truly disciples of Mine; and you will know the truth, and the truth will make you free...Truly, truly, I say to you, everyone who commits sin is the slave of sin. The slave does not remain in the house forever; the Son does remain forever. So if the Son makes you free, you will be free indeed." (Jn 8:31–32, 34-36 NIV) Later, Rabbi Paul wrote to the Galatians, "What the Messiah has freed us for is freedom! Therefore, stand firm, and don't let yourselves be tied up again to a yoke of slavery." (Ga 5:1 CJB)

WHAT YOU WILL NEED

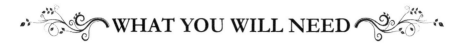

The Bible requires at least three elements to celebrate Passover: a Sacrifice Lamb, Unleavened Bread, and Bitter Herbs. (Ex 12:8). Today we have more elements that help tell the story of Passover.

Your table should include:

1. A **Seder Plate** that has:
    - A lamb shank-bone
    - A bitter herb (or 2)
    - Charoset
    - Parsley

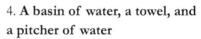

2. Enough **matzah** for your group
3. **Saltwater** for dipping

4. **A basin of water, a towel, and a pitcher of water**

5. Linen or cloth **napkin** on a plate that can hold **three matzah**

6. **A glass for each person** to drink four cups of wine or grape juice during the Seder

7. **An extra place** setting of wine glass for Elijah the Prophet

8. Some choose to prepare a **Lamb** dish according to Exodus 12; others use the shank bone to represent the sacrifice.

9. Special effects for the plagues and blood on the doorposts

Everything that is prepared should be without leaven.

CLEANING OUT THE LEAVEN

 We remove the leaven from our homes before the Seder meal and prepare for the Feast of Unleavened bread. This project is an excellent job for the whole family. Go through the ingredients in all the food showing the children "hidden" leaven (For example, often hot sauce has yeast in it). After removing the leaven, keep one piece to bring outside before the seder meal starts. We think it works best if you have one obvious (like pizza) and one "hidden" example. This way, you can talk about the sin that is hard to find in our lives.

DOORPOSTS CRAFT

Before you come back in from removing the leaven, it is a great craft to come up with a way to simulate the blood on the doorposts. It is a reminder of the themes of Passover and a testimony to anyone who walks by your home. Be creative. Here are some ideas on what we have done.

1. Red Paper or pre-painted with red paint, then water is used to "paint" the door as people come to the meal.
2. Red lights that you can turn on during the meal.
3. Red streamers or scarves

SPECIAL EFFECTS FOR THE PLAGUES

Effects take some preparation, but this is a fun and memorable part of the meal. We suggest buying some plastic frogs, bugs, golf balls (for hail), etc. You can use these as props during the portion of Seder, maybe even throwing them at each other as the plagues come up in the story. Surprising your guests will make it very memorable. Remember that some plagues only happen to the Egyptians so be aware as you explain it to your group. The most important thing is to make it memorable!

CELEBRATING THE
PASSOVER SEDER

CLEANING OUT THE LEAVEN (HAMETZ)

Leader: Seven days you shall eat unleavened bread, but on the first day, you shall remove leaven from your houses; for whoever eats anything leavened from the first day until the seventh day, that person shall be cut off from Israel" (Ex 12:15 NASB).

BARUCH ATAH ADONAI, ELOHEINU MELECH HAOLAM, ASHER KID'SHANU B'MITZVOTAV V'TZIVANU AL BI'UR CHAMETZ.	בָּרוּךְ אַתָּה יהוה, אֱלֹהֵינוּ, מֶלֶךְ הָעוֹלָם אֲשֶׁר קִדְּשָׁנוּ בְּמִצְוֹ תָיו, וְצִוָּנוּ עַל בְּעוּר חָמֵץ.

BLESSED ARE YOU, LORD OUR GOD, KING OF THE UNIVERSE, WHO SANCTIFIED US WITH HIS COMMANDMENTS AND COMMANDS US TO REMOVE CHAMETZ.

"Your boasting is not good. Don't you know the saying, "It takes only a little hametz to leaven a whole batch of dough?" Get rid of the old hametz, so that you can be a new batch of dough, because in reality you are unleavened. For our Pesach lamb, the Messiah, has been sacrificed. So let us celebrate the Seder not with leftover hametz, the hametz of wickedness and evil, but with the matzah of purity and truth." (1 Co 5:6–8 CJB)

PAINTING THE DOORPOSTS

Leader: let's go to the door and make sure that we all see the blood on the doorpost. Everyone paints some "blood" on the doorpost.

Everyone reads together:
"When your son asks you in time to come, saying 'What are the testimonies and the statutes and the ordinances that Adonai our

God commanded you?' then you are to tell your Son, 'We were slaves to Pharaoh in Egypt, and Adonai brought us out from Egypt with a mighty hand. Before our eyes Adonai showed signs and wonders, great and terrible—on Egypt, on Pharaoh, and on all his house. Then He brought us out from there so that He might bring us in, to give us the land that He swore to our fathers." (Duet 6:20-23 TLV)

TELLING THE STORY WITH QUESTIONS

The Leader says: Already this meal should seem different. As we go, you might want to ask some questions like:

1. Why do we dip parsley in saltwater?
2. Why do we only eat matzah?
3. Why do we eat bitter herbs?
4. Why do we only eat roasted lamb?

4 QUESTIONS (MA NISHTANA מה נשתנה)

Traditionally the youngest child asks (or sings):

MAH NISHTANAH,
HALAYLAH HA-ZEH,
MIKOL HALEYLOT

מַה נִּשְׁתַּנָה,
הַלַּיְלָה הַזֶּה
מִכָּל הַלֵּילוֹת

WHY IS THIS NIGHT DIFFERENT FROM ALL OTHER NIGHTS?

The traditional song is in the appendix.

Leader:

Passover is also considered a Holy Convocation and a Sabbath. (Lev 23) God tells us that one of the reasons we can rest on the Sabbath is because He freed us from Egypt (Ex 20:8-11). So traditionally, we set aside this time in three ways; lighting sabbath candles, thanking God for the season and drinking the first cup of our meal: the cup of sanctification.

LIGHTING CANDLES

Light the **Shabbat candles** and say **either**:
This is the traditional blessing for the candles

BARUCH ATAH ADONAI, ELOHEINU MELECH HA'OLAM, ASHER KID'SHANU B'MITZVOTAV V'TZIVANU L'HADLIK NER SHEL SHABBAT.	בָּרוּךְ אַתָּה יהוה, אֱלֹהֵינוּ מֶלֶךְ הָעוֹלָם, אֲשֶׁר קִדְּשָׁנוּ בְּמִצְוֹתָיו, וְצִוָּנוּ לְהַדְלִיק נֵר שֶׁל שַׁבָּת

"BLESSED ARE YOU, LORD OUR GOD, KING OF THE UNIVERSE, WHO SANCTIFIED US WITH HIS COMMANDMENTS AND COMMANDED US TO LIGHT THE SHABBAT CANDLES."

Or, since there is no commandment in the Bible to light Sabbath or Holiday lights, many use this blessing instead:

BARUCH ATAH ADONAI, ELOHEINU MELECH HA'OLAM ASHER KIDD'SHANU BEMITZVATOV V'TSIVANU LIHEYOT OR LAGOYIM V'NATAN-LANU ET YESHUA MESHICHEINU OR HAOLAM.	בָּרוּךְ אתָּה יהוה, אֱלֹהֵינוּ מֶלֶךְ הָעוֹלָם, אֲשֶׁר קִדְּשָׁנוּ בְּמִצְוֹתָיו וְצִוָּנוּ לִהְיוֹת אוֹר לַגּוֹיִים נָתַן לָנוּ אֶת יֵשׁוּעַ מְשִׁיחֵנוּ

"BLESSED ARE YOU, LORD OUR GOD, KING OF THE UNIVERSE, WHO HAS SANCTIFIED US WITH HIS COMMANDMENTS, AND COMMANDED US TO BE A LIGHT TO THE NATIONS, AND WHO GAVE TO US YESHUA OUR MESSIAH, THE LIGHT OF THE WORLD."

"Yeshua spoke to them again: 'I am the light of the world; whoever follows me will never walk in darkness but will have the light which gives life.'"
-John 8:12 (CJB)

1ST CUP THE CUP OF SANCTIFICATION

The Leader holds up a cup of wine (or juice) and says :

BARUKH ATA ADONAI,
ELOHEINU MELEKH
HA-OLAM, BOREI PERI
HAGAFEN.

בָּרוּךְ אַתָּה יהוה
אֱלֹהֵינוּ מֶלֶךְ
הָעוֹלָם בּוֹרֵא פְּרִי
הַגָּפֶן

"BLESSED ARE YOU, LORD OUR GOD, KING OF
THE UNIVERSE, WHO CREATES THE FRUIT OF THE
VINE."

Leader says: "In ancient times, only free people could relax
while eating a meal. Since God has set up free, let's lean
together."

 Encourage the kids to slump in their seats, put their
elbows on the table, and lean in a silly way.

BLESSING THE SEASON (SHECHEYANU שהחיינו)

Leader says:

BARUCH ATAH ADONAI,
ELOHEINU MELECH
HA'OLAM,
SHEHECHEYANU,
V'KIY'MANU, V'HIGIYANU
LAZ'MAN HAZEH.

בָּרוּךְ אַתָּה יהוה,
אֱלֹהֵינוּ מֶלֶךְ,
הָעוֹלָם,
שֶׁהֶחֱיָנוּ
וְקִיְּמָנוּ וְהִגִּיעָנוּ
לִזְמַן הַזֶּה.

"BLESSED ARE YOU, *LORD* OUR GOD, KING OF THE
UNIVERSE, WHO GRANTED US LIFE, SUSTAINED US,
AND BROUGHT US TO THIS SEASON.

WASHING HANDS (Urchatz ורחץ)

The Leader reads: Before running water was
available in most homes, hand-washing was
done with a pitcher and a basin. This tradition
may seem strange because we have plumbing
and bathrooms. But, hand-washing also has a
connection to the basin in the temple which
the LORD told Moses to tell Aaron to "wash
their hands and feet." (Exodus 30:19) The
Rabbi's extended this commandment onto
hand-washing called Netilat Yadayim. In
tradition. This kind of washing is done before every meal, after
the bathroom, after sleeping, etc. It is referred to in the Talmud
almost 350 times. This means that this tradition happens a lot.

So at Passover, one would expect to wash at least before the
meal. However, in an attempt to cause a child to ask questions,
it became the tradition to wash hands at the "wrong" time (right
after the first cup) without saying the blessing.

Similarly, Yeshua famously changed the usual routine at his last
Passover Meal by stoping to wash the disciple's feet; perhaps he
was thinking about the temple in the same way.

"So after He had washed their feet and put His robe back on and
reclined again, He said to them, He said to them, 'Do you
understand what I have done for you? You call Me 'Teacher' and
'Master'—and rightly you say, for I am. So if I, your Master and
Teacher, have washed your feet, you also ought to wash each
other's feet." (John 13:12-14 TLV)

Leader: Stand taking the basin over to one of the children.
Ask them to wash your feet but then wash theirs instead.

Pick someone to read each part of the story:

Reader:

"Joseph died, and all his brothers and all that generation. But the sons of Israel were fruitful and increased greatly, and multiplied, and became exceedingly mighty, so that the land was filled with them. Now a new king arose over Egypt, who did not know Joseph. He said to his people, "Behold, the people of the sons of Israel are more and mightier than we. "Come, let us deal wisely with them, or else they will multiply and in the event of war, they will also join themselves to those who hate us, and fight against us and depart from the land." So they appointed taskmasters over them to afflict them with hard labor. And they built for Pharaoh storage cities, Pithom and Raamses." (Ex 1:6–11 NASB).

PARSLEY & SALTWATER (KARPAS כרפס)

 The Leader picks up parsley and asks the children if they ordered an appetizer. Explain that we have a special appetizer tonight. Have everyone dip their parsley in saltwater.

The Leader says:

BARUCH ATAH ADONAI, ELOHEINU MELECH HA'OLAM, BOREI P'RI HA'ADAMAH.	בָּרוּךְ אַתָּה יהוה אֱלֹהֵינוּ מֶלֶךְ הָעוֹלָם, בּוֹרֵא פְּרִי הָאֲדָמָה

BLESSED ARE YOU, LORD, OUR GOD, RULER OF THE UNIVERSE, WHO CREATES THE FRUIT OF THE EARTH.

The Leader asks: How does this appetizer taste? Have you ever cried so hard you could tase it? What kind of story do you think this will be?

The Leader explains: "The saltwater reminds us of our tears, and the parsley reminds us of the hyssop used to paint the doorposts of the house. But Pharaoh kept making it worse."

Reader: 'The people of Israel groaned because of their slavery and cried out for help. Their cry for rescue from slavery came up to God." (Exodus 2:23-24 ESV)

Reader:
"But the more they afflicted them, the more they multiplied and the more they spread out, so that they were in dread of the sons of Israel." (Ex 1:12 NASB)

The Leader explains: But God helped us continue growing despite the brutal persecution. So Pharaoh came up with a new idea to kill the baby boys.

Reader:
Then Pharaoh gave this order to all his people: "Every Hebrew boy that is born you must throw into the Nile, but let every girl live." (Exodus 1:22 NIV)

BITTER HERBS (MAROR מרור)

BARUCH ATAH ADONAI, ELOHEINU MELECH HA'OLAM, ASHER KID'SHANU B'MITZVOTAV V'TZIVANU AL A-CHILAT MA-ROR	בָּרוּךְ אַתָּה יהוה אֱלֹהֵינוּ מֶלֶךְ הָעוֹלָם אֲשֶׁר קִדְּשָׁנוּ בְּמִצְוֹתָיו וְצִוָּנוּ עַל אֲכִילַת מָרוֹר

BLESSED ARE YOU, LORD, OUR GOD, RULER OF THE UNIVERSE, WHO SANCTIFIED US WITH HIS COMMANDMENTS AND COMMANDED US TO EAT BITTER HERBS.

"That night, they are to eat the meat roasted in the fire; they are to eat it with matzah and maror." (Ex 12:8 CJB).

The Leader explains: But, even in the middle of our sadness and the bitter cruelty of our slave masters, God had a plan of deliverance.

Reader:

"Now a man from the house of Levi took as his wife a daughter of Levi. The woman conceived and gave birth to a son. Now

when she saw that he was delightful, she hid him for three months. But when she could no longer hide him, she took a basket of papyrus reeds, coated it with tar and pitch, put the child inside, and laid it in the reeds by the bank of the Nile." (Exodus 2:1-3 TLV)

The Leader explains:

This deliverer was named Moses, which means "because I drew him out of the water ."Pharaoh had tried to kill us, but instead, God provided someone who would lead us out of slavery.

Reader:

"During those many days the king of Egypt died, and the people of Israel groaned because of their slavery and cried out for help. Their cry for rescue from slavery came up to God. And God heard their groaning, and God remembered his covenant with Abraham, with Isaac, and with Jacob. God saw the people of Israel—and God knew." (Ex 2:23-25 ESV)

The Leader explains:

So God called Moses to go to Pharaoh and lead us out of Egypt.

Reader:

"And now, behold, the cry of the sons of Israel has come to Me; furthermore, I have seen the oppression with which the Egyptians are oppressing them. And now come, and I will send you to Pharaoh, so that you may bring My people, the sons of Israel, out of Egypt." (Ex 3:10 NASB)

Reader:

"But I know that the king of Egypt will not let you go unless a mighty hand compels him. So I will stretch out my hand and strike the Egyptians with all the wonders that I will perform among them. After that, he will let you go." (Ex 3:19-20 NIV)

Reader:

After that, Moshe and Aharon came and said to Pharaoh, "Here is what Adonai, the God of Isra'el, says: 'Let my people go, so that they can celebrate a festival in the desert to honor me.'" (Exodus 5:1 CJB)

Reader:

"Then on the same day Pharaoh commanded the slave masters of the people and their foremen saying, "You are not to give the people any more straw to make bricks, as before. Let them go and gather straw for themselves. But impose on them the quota of bricks that they made previously; don't reduce it. For they are lazy—that's why they cry out saying, 'Let us go and sacrifice to our God.'" (Ex 5:6-8 TLV)

CHAROSET (חרוסת)

Leader:

The mixture of fruit and nuts help us to remember the mortar from the bricks we had to make the Egyptian cities. It reminds us that Pharaoh hardened His heart towards God and made it worse for us. Because of this, God told Moses that Pharaoh would only hear if God made him listen.

Reader emphasizing the bold words:

"Therefore, say to the Israelites: 'I am the Lord, and **I will bring you** out from under the yoke of the Egyptians. **I will free you** from being slaves to them, and **I will redeem you** with an outstretched arm and with mighty acts of judgment. **I will take you as my own people**, and I will be your God. **Then you will know that I am the Lord** your God, who brought you out from under the yoke of the Egyptians." (Ex 6:6-7 NIV)

Reader:

"When Pharaoh does not listen to you, then I will lay My hand on Egypt and bring out My hosts, My people the sons of Israel, from the land of Egypt by great judgments. **The Egyptians shall know that I am the Lord**, when I stretch out My hand on Egypt and bring out the sons of Israel from their midst." (Ex 7:4–5 NASB).

THE PLAGUES OF EGYPT

All Together:

"I declare today to the Lord your God that I have come to the land the Lord swore to our ancestors to give us…My father was a wandering Aramean, and he went down into Egypt with a few people and lived there and became a great nation, powerful and numerous."But the Egyptians mistreated us and made us suffer, subjecting us to harsh labor. Then we cried out to the Lord, the God of our ancestors, and the Lord heard our voice and saw our misery, toil and oppression. So the Lord brought us out of Egypt with a mighty hand and an outstretched arm, with great terror and with signs and wonders." (Deut 26:3, 5-8)

Leader:

Please take the next cup, the cup of deliverance, and ask each person to dip their finger, reducing one drop at a time as we go over each plague. Each time God brought a plague on Egypt, he had Moses tell him to "let my people go," but each time, the answer was no. I will say the Hebrew name, and you can repeat it in English. Don't lick your finger!

This is a great time to use those props you collected. Make it fun, don't worry if it makes a mess!

 Dam (Blood) Water was changed to blood.

 Tzefardeyah (Frogs) Frogs sprang up

 Kinim (Gnats) – On all animals and People

 Arov (Flies) Flies in Egypt but not in Goshen

 Dever (Pestilence) – A plague killed off the Egyptian livestock but not for the Israelites

 Sh'chin (Boils) – An epidemic of boils afflicted the Egyptians but not the Israelites

 Barad (Hail) – Hail destroyed the crops but not in Goshen.

 Arbeh (Locusts) – Locusts swarmed over Egypt, but not on the crops of the Israelites.

 Choshech (Darkness) – Egypt was covered in thick darkness like the darkness at creation. But not in Goshen.

THE PASSOVER LAMB (QORBAN PESAḤ קרבן פסח)

Leader:

Between the darkness and the last plague, God set apart this day as a holy day, a day to remember what he did to Egypt, but also a day that becomes a central theme throughout the entire Bible.

 Like the doorposts, if we are covered by the blood of the sacrifice of the Lamb, death passes us over! It is the cure for the bitterness of slavery, the answer to the affliction of our sin, and it starts a new life of freedom!

Reader: "This month is to be for you the first month, the first month of your year. Tell the whole community of Israel that on the tenth day of this month each man is to take a lamb for his family, one for each household." (Ex 12:2–3 NIV)

Reader:

"That night, they are to eat the meat, roasted in the fire; they are to eat it with matzah and maror." (Ex 12:8 CJB)

Reader:

"Here is how you are to eat it: with your belt fastened, your shoes on your feet and your staff in your hand; and you are to eat it hurriedly. It is Adonai's Pesach [Passover]. For that night, I will pass through the land of Egypt and kill all the firstborn in the land of Egypt, both men and animals; and I will execute judgment against all the gods of Egypt; I am Adonai. The blood will serve you as a sign marking the houses where you are; when I see the blood, I will pass over you - when I strike the land of Egypt, the death blow will not strike you. This will be a day for you to remember and celebrate as a festival to Adonai; from generation to generation you are to celebrate it by a perpetual regulation." (Ex 12:11-14 CJB)

Leader:

This pattern is also seen in the writings of the Hebrew prophets when they were describing the Messiah. For example in Isaiah, it says:

Reader:

"Who has believed our report? To whom is the arm of Adonai revealed? For He grew up before Him like a tender shoot, like a root out of dry ground. He had no form or majesty that we should look at Him, nor beauty that we should desire Him. He was despised and rejected by men, a man of sorrows, acquainted with grief, One from whom people hide their faces. He was despised, and we did not esteem Him. Surely He has borne our griefs and carried our pains. Yet we esteemed Him stricken, struck by God, and afflicted. But He was pierced because of our transgressions, crushed because of our iniquities. The chastisement for our shalom was upon Him, and by His stripes we are healed. We all like sheep have gone astray. Each of us turned to his own way. So Adonai has laid on Him the iniquity of us all. He was oppressed and He was afflicted yet He did not open His mouth. Like a lamb led to the slaughter, like a sheep before its shearers is silent, so He did not open His mouth. (Isa 53:1-7 TLV)

Leader:

Perhaps this is what John was thinking about when he said when he saw Yeshua coming to be baptized in the Jordan river, "Look, the Lamb of God, who takes away the sin of the world! This is the one I meant when I said, 'A man who comes after me has surpassed me because he was before me.' I myself did not know him, but the reason I came baptizing with water was that he might be revealed to Israel." (Jn 1:29–31 NIV)

Later, Rabbi Paul puts all these ideas together in a letter to the primarily Gentile congregation in Corinth. "Your boasting is not good. Don't you know the saying, "It takes only a little hametz to leaven a whole batch of dough?" Get rid of the old hametz, so that you can be a new batch of dough, because in reality you are unleavened. For our Pesach lamb, the Messiah, has been sacrificed. So let us celebrate the Seder not with leftover hametz, the hametz of wickedness and evil, but with the matzah of purity and truth." (1 Co 5:6–8 CJB)

Leader: The Lamb of God is the deliverance from the judgments from God.

Moses writes, "Now when it happens that your children ask you, 'What does this ceremony mean to you?' You are to say, 'It is the sacrifice of Adonai's Passover, because He passed over the houses of Bnei-Yisrael in Egypt, when He struck down the Egyptians, but spared our households.' So the people bowed their heads and worshipped." (Ex 12:26–27 TLV)

But for Eygpt, there was one final and terrible plague.

10. Makkat Bechorot (killing of the firstborn)

 Pause for a moment and ask the room how many firstborns there are at the table. Take a moment to point out who would be missing if God hadn't delivered us.

THE MATZAH (YACHATZ יחץ)

Leader: The following day, Pharaoh and the people of Egypt were eager to let us go.

Reader:
The Egyptians pressed to send the people out of the land quickly because they said, "Otherwise, we'll all be dead!" The people took their dough before it had become leavened and

wrapped their kneading bowls in their clothes on their shoulders. (Ex 12:33–34 CJB)

The Leader holds up the three matzahs and says:
"What do these three matzah represent? Some say they represent Abraham, Issac, and Jacob. But Issac is never broken? What do you think it represents?"

 The Leader then breaks the middle matzah, wraps it in a cloth, and hides it o be found after the meal. Ask the kids, "why do we break the middle matzah and hide it to be redeemed later?"

Reader:
"You shall not eat leavened bread with it; for seven days you shall eat unleavened bread with it, the bread of affliction (for you came out of the land of Egypt in a hurry), so that you will remember the day when you came out of the land of Egypt all the days of your life." (Dt 16:3 NASB)

2ND CUP: CUP OF DELIVERANCE

The Leader takes the cup that was reduced and say this blessing:

BARUKH ATA ADONAI, ELOHEINU MELEKH HA-OLAM, BOREI PERI HAGAFEN.	בָּרוּךְ אַתָּה יהוה אֱלֹהֵינוּ מֶלֶךְ הָעוֹלָם בּוֹרֵא פְּרִי הַגָּפֶן

"BLESSED ARE YOU, LORD OUR GOD, KING OF THE UNIVERSE, WHO CREATES THE FRUIT OF THE VINE."

All Together:
"We were slaves but now we are free!"

Drink the second cup

IT WOULD HAVE BEEN ENOUGH

I - lu ho - tzi ho - tzi - a - nu, ho - tzi - a - nu mi - mitz - ra - yim,

ho - tzi - a - nu mi - mitz - ra - yim da - yei - nu.

(Chorus) Da - da - yei - nu,___ da - da - yei - nu,___ da - da - yei - nu, da -

yei - nu da - yei - nu da - yei - nu. yei - nu da - yei - nu.

(DAYENU דינו)

v'lo natan natan lanu, natan lanu et hashabbat (The Sabbath)

v'lo natan natan lanu, natan lanu et hatorah, (The Torah)

v'lo natan natan lanu, natan lanu et Yeshua, (Jesus)

THE MEAL: (SHULCHAN OREICH שלחן עורך)

Leader: Pray for the meal in light of the story

Leader: As we are eating, try some fun things like:
- Go around the table and ask people to share something that happened in the last year that would have been enough, but God did even more.
  - Everyone replies DAYENU!
- Mix all the elements. Rabbi Hillel took the scripture literally and put the lamb, bitter herbs, and matzah together into what is now known as a Hillel sandwich.
- Have a bitter herb contest, but be careful!

DURING THE MEAL

Leader: During Messiah's Passover Meal, the gospel of Matthew records Yeshua saying, "He who dipped his hand with Me in the bowl is the one who will betray Me." (Mt 26:23 NASB). This means He was emphasizing the bitterness and tears associated with this betrayal.

ELIJAH THE PROPHET

Leader: Elijah is not a part of the Exodus story, but he is an important tradition in the Passover Seder. Malachi said, "I will send my messenger, who will prepare the way before me. Then suddenly the Lord you are seeking will come to his temple; the messenger of the covenant, whom you desire, will come," says the Lord Almighty." (Mal 3:1) Mark tells us that this was the reason John the Baptist came to fulfill this prophecy. (Mark 1:1-4) Yeshua tells us, "And if you are willing to accept it, he is the Elijah who was to come. Whoever has ears, let them hear." (Matthew 11:14 NIV)

For us this means Elijah has already come and Messiah Yeshua after him. When John was in the wilderness baptizing people in the Jordan river he said about Yeshua, "Behold, the Lamb of God, who takes away the sin of the world!" (John1:29 ESV)

Have a child check the door to see if Elijah is at the door.

"Elijah was a man with a nature like ours, and he prayed earnestly that it might not rain. And it did not rain on the earth for three years and six months. He prayed again, and the sky gave rain, and the earth produced its fruit. My brothers and sisters, if any among you strays from the truth and someone turns him back, let him know that the one who turns a sinner from the error of his way shall save a soul from death and cover a multitude of sins." (James 4:17-19 TLV)

AFTER THE MEAL: (AFIKOMEN אפיקומן) 🎋

Have the children search for the Afikomen. Then redeem it by negotiating a price.

Leader: This exchange is based on the redemption of the firstborn after the Exodus. God required a price for our lives by exchanging our lives for the life of the Passover Lamb. Yeshua gave up His life on Passover in an even more dramatic way as the Passover Lamb for our redemption. Towards the end of the meal, Yeshua took the bread and blessed it.

BARUKH ATA ADONAI,	בָּרוּךְ אַתָּה יהוה
ELOHEINU MELEKH	אֱלֹהֵינוּ מֶלֶךְ
HA-OLAM, HAMOTZI	הָעוֹלָם הַמּוֹצִיא
LECHEM MIN HAARETZ	לֶחֶם מִן הָאָרֶץ.

"BLESSED ARE YOU, LORD OUR GOD, KING OF THE UNIVERSE, WHO BRINGS FORTH BREAD FROM THE EARTH."

Leader: Then he added, "This is my body, which is for you; do this in remembrance of me." (1 Co 11:24 NIV)

So Yeshua is saying that the Afikomen, the middle matzah (broken, hidden, and redeemed), actually represented Him. As a fulfillment of Old Testament Prophecy, He would be our Passover lamb. Yeshua died on the cross later that day; His brokenness is our redemption. So He calls us to remember him every time we celebrate the story of Passover. This was such a powerful image that the disciples and followers of Yeshua quickly made it part of their communal meals.[1]

Take the Afikomen and share it with each person at the table.

---

[1] https://www.biblicalarchaeology.org/daily/biblical-topics/bible-interpretation/when-was-the-first-communion/

3RD CUP: THE CUP OF REDEMPTION

Leader: After Yeshua shared the bread, he also lifted the cup of redemption

BARUKH ATA ADONAI, ELOHEINU MELEKH HA-OLAM, BOREI PERI HAGAFEN.

בָּרוּךְ אַתָּה יהוה
אֱלֹהֵינוּ מֶלֶךְ
הָעוֹלָם בּוֹרֵא פְּרִי
הַגָּפֶן

"BLESSED ARE YOU, LORD OUR GOD, KING OF THE UNIVERSE, WHO CREATES THE FRUIT OF THE VINE."

Leader:

"And He took a cup; and after giving thanks, He gave to them, saying, "Drink from it, all of you; for this is My blood of the covenant, which is poured out for many for the removal of sins. But I say to you, I will never drink of this fruit of the vine from now on, until that day when I drink it anew with you in My Father's kingdom." (Matthew 26:27-28 TLV)

Yeshua's declaration is a fulfillment of the prophet Jeremiah 31:31.

"Behold, days are coming," declares the Lord, "when I will make a new covenant with the house of Israel and with the house of Judah, not like the covenant which I made with their fathers in the day I took them by the hand to bring them out of the land of Egypt, My covenant which they broke, although I was a husband to them," declares the Lord. But this is the covenant which I will make with the house of Israel after those days," declares the Lord, "I will put My law within them and on their heart I will write it; and I will be their God, and they shall be My people." (Je 31:31–33 NASB)

YESHUA OUR SACRIFICIAL LAMB

Leader:

Later that day Yeshua was arrested and crucified on a Roman cross. In fulfillment of prophecy, He then took the bitterness of our slavery to sin on himself by being our Passover lamb, the bread of affliction, and redeeming us by his blood. This means if we put our trust in Him, then He is our God, and we are His people. Just like the blood over the door, Yeshua's blood cover us and if we put our trust in Him death passes us over.

FIRST FRUITS & RESURRECTION

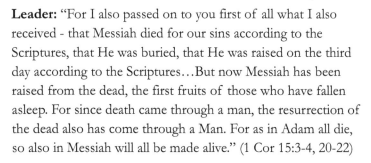

Leader: "For I also passed on to you first of all what I also received - that Messiah died for our sins according to the Scriptures, that He was buried, that He was raised on the third day according to the Scriptures...But now Messiah has been raised from the dead, the first fruits of those who have fallen asleep. For since death came through a man, the resurrection of the dead also has come through a Man. For as in Adam all die, so also in Messiah will all be made alive." (1 Cor 15:3-4, 20-22)

Leader: What Yeshua did not only saved us, but it also means that if we put our trust in Him we can live in the power of His resurrection.

"Behold, I tell you a mystery: We shall not all sleep, but we shall all be changed- in a moment, in the twinkling of an eye, at the last shofar. For the shofar will sound, and the dead will be raised incorruptible, and we will be changed." (1 Cor 15:51-52)

All together:

"Death is swallowed up in victory. Where, O Death, is your victory? Where, O Death, is your sting?" (1 Cor 15:55)

4TH CUP: THE CUP OF PRAISE

Leader: The cup of praise becomes our future. We are waiting for the day of Yeshua's kingdom on earth when He will drink the cup of praise together with His people.

It is traditional to sing or read The Hallel (Praise) Psalms after the meal. We see this tradition clearly as the disciples sing a hymn on their way to the Mount of Olives after their meal. (Matt 26:30, Mark 14:26). Psalm 118 is one of the Hallel Psalms.

Reader:
"I will give you thanks, for you answered me; you have become my salvation. The stone the builders rejected has become the cornerstone; the Lord has done this, and it is marvelous in our eyes. The Lord has done it this very day; let us rejoice today and be glad." (Psalm 118:21-24) Yeshua claimed that this Psalm referred to Him and His death in a parable in Mark 12.

In the Book of Revelation, John sees a vision of the Messiah sitting on the throne in heaven, as a lamb "as if it were slain ." The Lamb is surrounded by creatures, elders, angels, Isreal, and an uncountable group of people from every nation. They are all worshiping the Lamb with songs giving Him glory and honor because of the power of His blood to redeem His people.

Paul writes that one day "that at the name of Yeshua every knee should bow, in heaven and on the earth and under the earth, and every tongue profess that Yeshua the Messiah is Lord - to the glory of God the Father." (Philippians 2:10-11 TLV)

Leader:
So let's lift the cup of praise as end our Seder looking forward to the return of our Passover Lamb, Yeshua the Messiah, our Lord.

BARUKH ATA ADONAI,
ELOHEINU MELEKH
HA-OLAM, BOREI PERI
HAGAFEN.

בָּרוּךְ אַתָּה יהוה
אֱלֹהֵינוּ מֶלֶךְ
הָעוֹלָם בּוֹרֵא פְּרִי
הַגָּפֶן

"BLESSED ARE YOU, LORD OUR GOD, KING OF THE UNIVERSE, WHO CREATES THE FRUIT OF THE VINE."

Leader: This is the end of our Seder
The leader can offer a spontaneous prayer for the whole group. Ending with looking foward to the return of our Prophet, Priest, and King Messiah: Yeshua

All together, we pray.

Next Year in Jerusalem!

APPENDIX:

THE FOUR QUESTIONS:

Mah nish-ta-nah ha - lay' lah ha-zeh mi - kol_ ha-lei - lot, mi - kol_ ha-lei - lot? She-b'

chol ha-lei-lot	a-nu och - lin cha - metz u-ma - tzah, cha - metz u-ma -
chol ha-lei-lot	a-nu och - lin sh' - ar_ y' - ra - kot, sh' - ar_ y' - ra -
chol ha-lei-lot ein	a-nu matbi lin a - fi-lu paam e - chat, a - fi-lu paam e -
chol ha-lei-lot	a-nu och - lin bein yosh-vin u - vein m' su- bin, bein yosh-vin u - vein m' su

tzah, ha - lay' lah ha-zeh, ha - lay' lah ha-zeh ku - lo___ ma - tzah,___ ha-
kot, ha - lay' lah ha-zeh, ha - lay' lah ha-zeh ma - ror,___ ma - ror,___ ha-
chat, ha - lay' lah ha-zeh, ha - lay' lah ha-zeh sh' - tei___ p' - a - mim,___ ha-
bin, ha - lay' lah ha-zeh, ha - lay' lah ha-zeh ku - la - nu m' - su - bin,___ ha-

lay'-lah ha - zeh, ha - lay'-lah ha-zeh ku - lo___ ma - tzah. She-b'
lay'-lah ha - zeh, ha - lay'-lah ha-zeh ma - ror,___ ma - ror. She-b'
lay'-lah ha - zeh, ha - lay'-lah ha-zeh sh' - tei___ p' - a - mim. She-b'
lay'-lah ha - zeh, ha - lay'-lah ha-zeh ku - la - nu m' - su - bin.

THE FEAST OF UNLEAVENED BREAD AND COUNTING THE OMER

This is only the beginning of this season. Passover is the first part of the feast of unleavened bread that then turns into counting the Omer, and then ends with Shavout (pentecost).

In the Torah God commands:
"From the day after the Sabbath, the day you brought the sheaf of the wave offering, count off seven full weeks. Count off fifty days up to the day after the seventh Sabbath, and then present an offering of new grain to the Lord." (Lev 23:15-16 NIV)

This is the same time that led us from Egypt to Mt. Sinai. It remind us of the giving of the Torah. Each day we thank God for his provisions by counting the Omer. The Omer is the measurement of daily provisions, or daily bread.

BARUKH ATA ADONAI,
ELOHEINU MELEKH
HA-OLAM,
ASHER KID'SHANU
B'MITZVOTAV
V'TIZIVANU AL SEFIRAT
HA'OMER.

בָּרוּךְ אַתָּה אֲדֹנָי
אֱלֹהֵינוּ מֶלֶךְ
הָעוֹלָם
אֲשֶׁר קִדְּשָׁנוּ
בְּמִצְוֹתָיו,
וְצִוָּנוּ עַל סְפִירַת
הָעֹמֶר.

"BLESSED ARE YOU, LORD OUR GOD, KING OF THE UNIVERSE, WHO COMMANDED US TO COUNT THE OMER.

After this blessing we say:
     Today is the _____ day of the omer.

Then we look forward to the anniversary of the pouring out of the Holy Spirit on the followers of Yeshua that enabled them to accomplish the work of telling the whole world of what Yeshua has done.

"When the day of Pentecost came, they were all together in one place. Suddenly a sound like the blowing of a violent wind came from heaven and filled the whole house where they were sitting. They saw what seemed to be tongues of fire that separated and came to rest on each of them. All of them were filled with the Holy Spirit and began to speak in other tongues as the Spirit enabled them." (Acts 2:1-4 NIV)

Made in the USA
Las Vegas, NV
10 April 2024